Kawaii Deco Sushi

カワイイデコ寿司

LITTLE MISS BENTO
SHIRLEY WONG

Marshall Cavendish
Cuisine

The publisher wishes to thank Topseller Pte Ltd for supplying the
Okome Shortgrain Rice used in this book and for supporting this book.

Editor: Lydia Leong
Designer: Bernard Go Kwang Meng
Photographer: Calvin Tan

Copyright © 2015 Marshall Cavendish International (Asia) Private Limited

Published by Marshall Cavendish Cuisine
An imprint of Marshall Cavendish International

Other Marshall Cavendish Offices:
Marshall Cavendish Corporation. 99 White Plains Road, Tarrytown NY 10591-9001, USA •
Marshall Cavendish International (Thailand) Co Ltd. 253 Asoke, 12th Floor, Sukhumvit 21 Road,
Klongtoey Nua, Wattana, Bangkok 10110, Thailand • Marshall Cavendish (Malaysia) Sdn Bhd,
Times Subang, Lot 46, Subang Hi-Tech Industrial Park, Batu Tiga, 40000 Shah Alam,
Selangor Darul Ehsan, Malaysia.

National Library Board, Singapore Cataloguing-in-Publication Data

Wong, Shirley, author.
Kawaii deco sushi / Shirley Wong. — Singapore : Marshall Cavendish Cuisine, 2015.
pages cm
ISBN : 978-981-4561-27-3 (paperback)

1. Cooking, Japanese. 2. Sushi. 3. Cookbooks. I. Title.

TX724.5.J3
641.5952 — dc23   OCN908676554

Printed in Singapore by Colourscan Print Co. Pte. Ltd.

Dedication

This book is for my mother
who laid the foundation
for my culinary adventures.

Acknowledgements

I would like to thank my family and closest friends for their constant support. It is only with their encouragement, that I found the strength to work on this second book.

I am also extremely grateful for the support of those who follow me on my social media platforms. To all of you, thank you for picking up this book. I am sure you will enjoy using this cookbook and trying out the step-by-step recipes inside.

A year ago, I would not have imagined that I would be writing and launching a second book in this Kawaii cookbook series so soon after the launch of the first, *Kawaii Bento*. To my editor, Lydia Leong and designer Benard Go, thank you for your patience and guidance, and for making the first book such a success. To my photographer, Calvin Tan, thank you for always making my food creations attractive in the photographs.

It took many long hours to put this book together, but every minute spent was worth it with your support. Thank you.

Contents

Introduction

Kazarimaki-sushi, translated as decorative sushi rolls or deco sushi, is a modern way of presenting sushi rolls in a highly creative way. It originated from the Boso Peninsula of Japan, where thick sushi rolls or *futo-maki* are common.

In this book, I'll show you how you can make your own deco sushi with the use and placement of various ingredients. And once you master the basics, you can start creating your own designs!

Deco sushi rolls are perfect for serving as finger food at parties, for bringing along to picnics, as well as for packing into bento boxes. What's more, these sushi rolls are not only tasty, they will delight, surprise and impress!

I have specially included detailed sections on basic tools and techniques, an illustrated glossary of ingredients, and step-by-step photographs with every recipe to guide you as you make these adorable sushi rolls.

Have fun making these *kawaii* (cute) deco sushi!

Shirley Wong
Little Miss Bento

Sushi Tools & Equipment

The following pages highlight some basic tools required for making deco sushi. Except for the sushi bamboo mat and *hangiri* wooden rice tub, the other items are general kitchen tools and equipment which you can find in most houseware shops and supermarkets.

Hangiri Wooden Rice Tub, Spatula and Fan

Although not essential, a *hangiri* (traditional flat-bottomed wooden tub), is useful for preparing sushi rice. A rice spatula is used to toss the cooked rice with the vinegar, sugar and salt mixture. A hand-held paper fan is used to cool the freshly-cooked rice as you toss it.

Digital Kitchen Weighing Scale

Making deco sushi requires precise measurements of the rice portions and other ingredients. A digital kitchen weighing scale will help ensure this.

Sushi Bamboo Mat

Sushi bamboo mats are available in various sizes. A large 30-cm x 25-cm mat is best for rolling the final sushi, while a smaller one would be more convenient for shaping and rolling the smaller parts of the sushi.

Knife

A specialised sushi knife or a
sharp kitchen knife is essential
for slicing sushi neatly. The
yanagiba, or willow-shaped
sushi knife (in the foreground)
is a specialised sushi/sashimi
knife designed to make
cutting sushi easier.

Cutting Board with Measurements

A cutting board with clearly marked units will
enable you to trim ingredients or cut the sushi
roll to the measurements required.

Lint-free Cloth

A lint-free cloth is a very useful item to have on
hand when making sushi. Wet, then wring it dry
and use it to pat the open end of the sushi roll to
compact the ingredients and keep the roll neat;
soften the seaweed before folding to prevent
tearing; and clean the knife to ensure neat and
clean cuts.

Cling Wrap

After measuring the portions of rice for your deco sushi, cover with cling wrap to prevent the rice from drying out while you work on the other parts of the recipe. Cling wrap is also useful for lining the sushi bamboo mat to prevent the rice from sticking to the mat when seaweed is not used. It can also be used to wrap the completed deco sushi.

Perforated Kitchen Gloves

Sometimes also known as sushi handling gloves, these perforated kitchen gloves are perfect for shaping and spreading the sticky sushi rice as it does not stick.

Kitchen Paper Towels

Paper towels are useful for patting dry sushi ingredients as sushi seaweed will tear if it is used to wrap ingredients that are too wet.

Typical Sushi Ingredients

Here are some of the common ingredients used in making deco sushi. Some ingredients can be found at local supermarkets and Japanese supermarkets, but other more specialised ingredients may only be available online. Feel free to substitute as necessary.

Sushi Seaweed

Sushi Rice Vinegar

Red Ginger / Pink Ginger

Pickled Burdock (*Yamagobo*)

Pickled Gourd Strips (*Kanpyo*)

Fried Tofu Pockets (*Aburaage*)

Ground Black Sesame (*Suri Goma*)

Marinated Seaweed (*Chuka Wakame*)

Dried Seaweed Powder (*Aosa*)

Dried Rice Topping
(*Furikake*)

Dehydrated Vegetable Powders

Fish Roe Powder
(*Mentaiko* Powder)

Flying Fish Roe (*Tobiko*)

Hard-boiled Egg Yolk

Grilled Omelette
(*Tamagoyaki*)

Sliced Cheese

Sliced Ham

Cheese, Meat and
Fish Sausages

Japanese Fish Roll
(*Kamaboko*)

Pink Fish Floss
(*Sakura Denbu*)

Pink Fish Flakes (*Oboro*)

About Sushi Rice

Sushi is typically made using Japanese or Japonica rice, a popular short-grain rice cultivated in Japan.

There are numerous varieties of Japonica rice and some of the more popular ones include Koshihikari, Sasanishiki and Akitakomachi.

While Japonica rice remains the best rice to use in terms of quality and taste for preparing authentic Japanese cuisine, other Japonica or Japonica hybrid rice are now available.

These rice varieties are cultivated in countries outside Japan and include Calrose, Kokuho Rose, Tamaki, Megumi, Hakura and Nishiki. These varieties usually taste reasonably close to Japan-grown rice and can be used in sushi-making. Their reasonable price tag also makes it easy for those on a budget.

Basic Sushi Techniques

COOKING SUSHI RICE

Ingredients

1 cup Japanese rice

180 ml mineral water

1$\frac{1}{2}$ Tbsp rice vinegar

1 Tbsp castor sugar

$\frac{1}{2}$ tsp salt

NOTE If using Japonica hybrid rice, increase the amount of cooking liquid by 5–10% as the grains tend to be drier.

Normal drinking water can be used to cook the rice, but using mineral water will make the cooked rice more fluffy and have a beautiful gleam.

1 cup raw rice will yield approximately 300 g cooked rice.

Method

Rinse the rice about three times. Do not rub the rice grains, but use your hand to swirl the water gently. Drain.

Add the mineral water to the rice and let soak for at least 30 minutes.

Cook the rice in a rice cooker according to the manufacturer's instructions.

When the rice is done, let rest for 15–20 minutes in the rice cooker before transferring to a *hangiri* wooden rice tub.

Mix the vinegar, sugar and salt together.

Add the vinegar mixture to the rice and mix with a spatula, using a gentle slicing action to avoid mashing the rice grains.

If the rice is too wet, fan the rice as you mix.

Mix until the vinegar is absorbed by the rice. The rice grains will be shiny. Set aside and cover with a damp, lint-free cloth.

HANDLING COOKED SUSHI RICE

Use peforated kitchen gloves when handling cooked sushi rice as the rice is less likely to stick to the gloves. Handle the rice lightly and gently with the tips of your fingers to avoid mashing the grains.

If handling the rice with bare hands, wet your hands intermittently to prevent sticking. Add about 1 tsp sushi rice vinegar to a small bowl of water and rub your hands with the water before handling the rice.

MEASURING COOKED SUSHI RICE

To form the various parts of a design, you will need to portion out the rice as specified in the recipe. After weighing the rice in the required portions, cover with cling wrap to prevent the rice from drying out.

SHAPING COOKED SUSHI RICE

Many recipes call for the rice to be arranged in mountains (think mountain ranges!). To do this, shape the portion of rice into a triangular strip about 10-cm long. Form the number of rice mountains directed in the recipe.

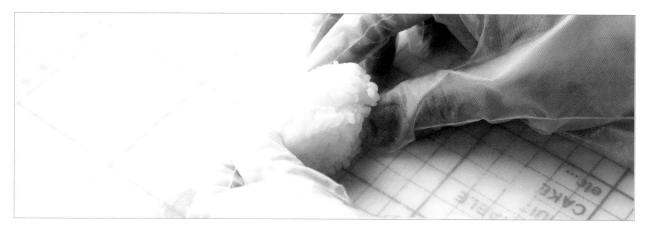

SPREADING SUSHI RICE ON SEAWEED

To make spreading the rice easier, divide the portion of rice into a few parts and space them out on the sheet of seaweed. Use your fingers to press and spread the rice evenly on the seaweed. For the final sushi roll to be even, spread the rice evenly to the edges of the seaweed, leaving a gap at one or both ends to seal the sushi roll.

SHAPING SUSHI ROLLS

Use the sushi bamboo mat to help you shape the roll.

Shaping a Round Sushi Roll
When making small round rolls, hold both ends of the sushi bamboo mat and move the roll from side to side to shape it evenly.

 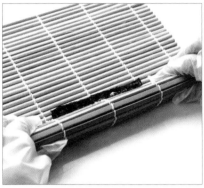 

Shaping a Teardrop Shape Roll

When making a teardrop shape roll, use the sushi bamboo mat to squeeze one side of the roll so it is sharper on one side.

Shaping the Final Sushi Roll

Hold the base firmly as you close up the sushi roll. Continue to tighten the roll to keep it compact. This is important for making neat sushi rolls. Once the roll is tight, gently press the sides using a damp lint-free cloth to further compact the roll.

CUTTING SUSHI ROLLS

It is best to use a specialised sushi knife to cut sushi rolls, but a sharp
kitchen knife makes a good substitute.

When cutting sushi rolls, do not push the knife down on the roll.
Instead, cut using a quick sawing motion parallel to your worktop.

The recipes in this book are meant for cutting
into 4 slices. Cut the sushi roll down the centre in
half, then halve each piece to obtain 4 slices. Do
note that deco sushi slices tend to be fairly large.

Clean the knife with a damp lint-free cloth
after each cut. Wipe away any ingredient
stains and rice grains, then wet the knife
to ensure neat and clean sushi slices.

COLOURING RICE

There are many ways to make colour cooked sushi rice to create the design you want. The table below offers some suggestions. Be creative!

Red	Ketchup	Marinated Fish Roe (*Mentaiko*)	Red Rice Topping (Red *Furikake*)			
Pink	Pink Rice Topping (Pink *Furikake*)	Salmon Flakes	Pink Fish Floss (*Sakura Denbu*)	Pink Sushi Mix	Pink Fish Flakes (*Oboro*)	
Yellow	Yellow Rice Topping (Yellow *Furikake*)	Mashed Hard-boiled Egg Yolk	Japanese Egg *Soboro*			
Orange	Fish Roe Soft Rice Topping (*Mentaiko* Soft *Furikake*)	Fish Roe Powder (*Mentaiko* Powder)	Prawn Roe (*Ebiko*)	Cod Roe Powder (*Tarako* Powder)	Salmon Soft Rice Topping (*Sake* Soft *Furikake*)	Dehydrated Carrot Powder
Green	Green Rice Topping (Green *Furikake*)	Boiled and Mashed Edamame Beans	Marinated Seaweed (*Chuka Wakame*)	Dehydrated Broccoli Powder	Dried Seaweed Powder (*Aosa*)	
Brown	Japanese Light Soy Sauce	Teriyaki Sauce	Cod Roe Soft Rice Topping (*Tarako* Soft *Furikake*)	Bonito Flakes Soft Rice Topping (*Okaka* Soft *Furikake*)	Roasted Soy Bean Rice Topping (*Kinako Furikake*)	Roasted White Sesame Powder
Purple	Purple Rice Topping (Purple *Furikake*)	Dried Red Perilla Mix (*Yukari*)	Chopped Purple Cabbage	Dehydrated Purple Sweet Potato Powder		
Blue	Blue Rice Topping (Blue *Furikake*)					
Black	Black Sesame Powder					

SUSHI SEAWEED 101

Supermarkets stock two sizes of sushi seaweed—the full-size (20.5-cm x 19-cm) and the half-size (19-cm x 9.5-cm). In this book, I use the half-size sheet, and refer to it as 1 sheet. If the half-size sheets are not available, get the full-size sheets and cut them in half.

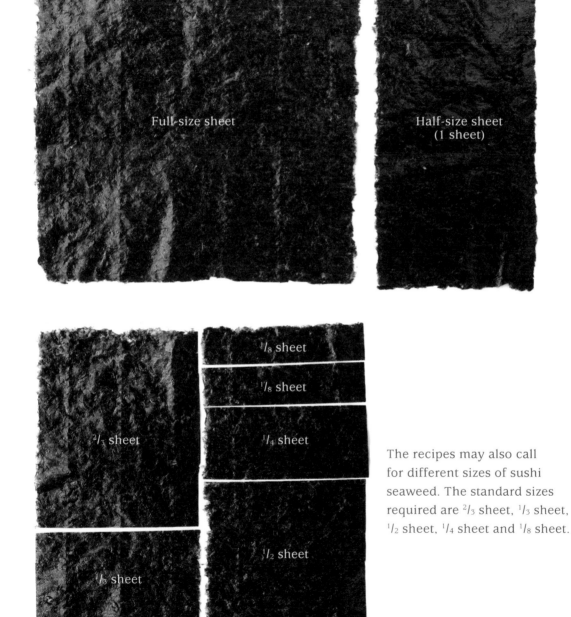

Full-size sheet

Half-size sheet
(1 sheet)

^{2}/$_3$ sheet

^{1}/$_3$ sheet

^{1}/$_8$ sheet

^{1}/$_8$ sheet

^{1}/$_4$ sheet

^{1}/$_2$ sheet

The recipes may also call for different sizes of sushi seaweed. The standard sizes required are ^{2}/$_3$ sheet, ^{1}/$_3$ sheet, ^{1}/$_2$ sheet, ^{1}/$_4$ sheet and ^{1}/$_8$ sheet.

Glossy side

Rough side

There are two sides to a sheet of sushi seaweed—the glossy side and the rough side. The glossy side should face outwards. Arrange the rice on the rough side.

Most of the recipes in this book require more than one sheet of sushi seaweed to enclose the design. This will be specified in the recipes. For example: 1 sheet + $^1/_3$ sheet, joined.
To join the sheets of sushi seaweed, stick them together by pressing a few grains of sushi rice on the edge of the sushi seaweed.

Some of the recipes in this book may require you to fold the sheet of sushi seaweed. To prevent the seaweed from breaking or tearing when folded, dab the folding line with a damp lint-free cloth.

When cutting seaweed, make a single cut through
with a sharp knife. Do not drag the knife across
the sheet as it would cause the seaweed to break.
Alternatively, use a pair of scissors to cut the seaweed.

MAKING PINK FISH FLAKES (OBORO)

Ingredients

240 g white flesh fish
(such as cod fish)

1 tsp salt

A little red food colouring

1 Tbsp Japanese sake

1 Tbsp castor sugar

1 tsp mirin

Method

Boil a pot of water and lower fish in to cook. When fish turns opaque, remove and drain well.

Peel off the skin and chop up the flesh. Remove any bones.

Using a *suribachi* (grinding mortar), grind the fish finely.

Wrap the fish using thin cooking gauze and rinse to remove the fish oil. Squeeze to remove excess water.

Place the fish in a bowl. Add red colouring, Japanese sake, sugar and mirin. Mix until fish is evenly coloured.

Heat a pan over medium-low heat and dry-fry fish until flaky and dry.

Set aside to cool before using.

MAKING A GRILLED OMELETTE (TAMAGOYAKI)

Ingredients

2 eggs

2 Tbsp dashi stock

1 tsp Japanese white soy sauce (*shiro shoyu*)

1 tsp sugar

cooking oil as needed

NOTE This recipe yields a small grilled omelette. For a larger omelette, adjust the portions.

Method

Beat the eggs in a measuring cup to facilitate the pouring of the egg later. Add the dashi stock, soy sauce and sugar and beat well to mix.

Heat a little oil in a *tamagoyaki* pan.

Pour a quarter of the egg mixture into the pan. Tilt the pan so the egg coats the base of the pan.

When the sides are cooked, roll the egg up from the other end towards the handle of the pan. Push the egg roll to the other side of the pan and pour in another quarter of the egg mixture. Repeat to cook and roll until the egg mixture is used up.

MAKING AN EGG SHEET

Ingredients

Eggs

NOTE Cook the beaten egg over very low heat to reduce bubbling. This will ensure that the egg sheet is smooth, evenly coloured and does not burn.

Method

Beat the eggs lightly.

Strain the beaten egg to remove any air bubbles.

Lightly oil a frying pan. Add the beaten egg to form a thin layer. Cover pan and cook over low heat.

When the egg sheet is about 80% done, turn off the heat and let the egg sheet sit for 20–30 seconds to finish cooking in the residual heat.

Remove from the pan, being careful not to tear the egg sheet. Use as desired.

Wrapping, Packing & Display Ideas

Deco sushi can be served as part of a regular meal, placed into bento boxes or packed into picnic baskets. Here are some suggestions on how you can wrap, pack and display deco sushi.

Arrange the deco sushi on a large plate to make a sushi centrepiece.

Pack the deco sushi in a bento box as part of a bento meal.

Pack the deco sushi in decorative food-grade plastic bags as a party goody bag item.

Place the deco sushi into small takeaway cups as party takeaway packs.

Wrap the deco sushi individually and take along for picnics.

33

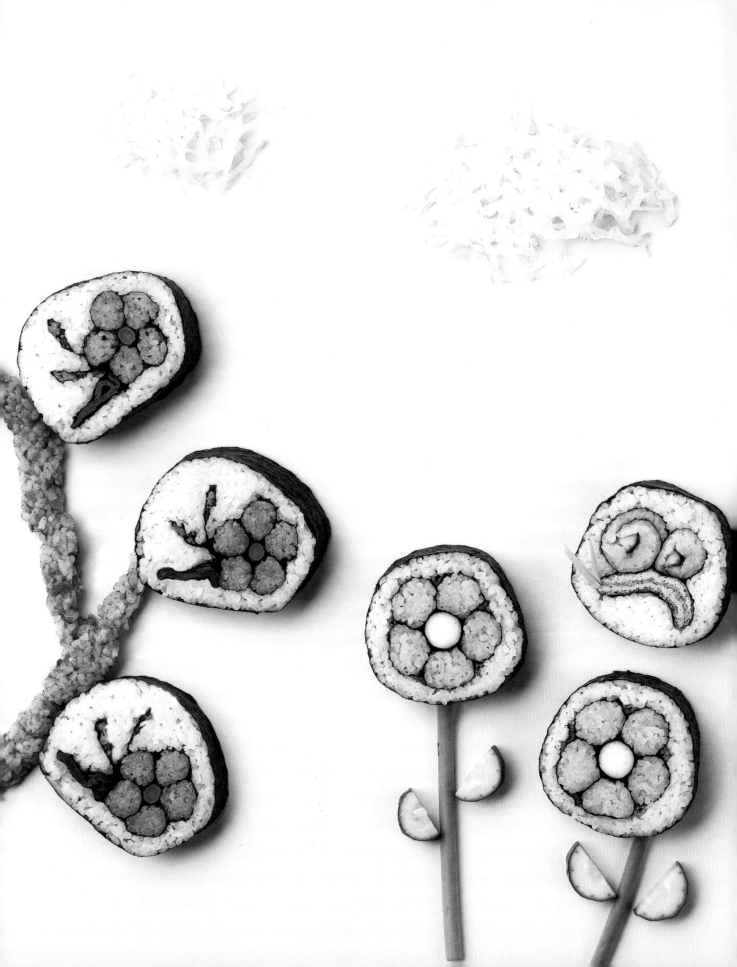

Garden Themed Sushi

Basic Flower お花

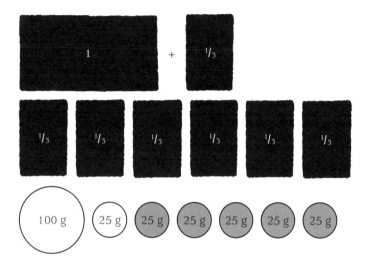

Ingredients

1 sheet + $^1/_3$ sheet of seaweed, joined

6 x $^1/_3$ sheet of seaweed

1 strip of seaweed, 10-cm x 1-cm

125 g white sushi rice, divided

125 g pink sushi rice (100 g white sushi rice + 25 g pink fish floss (*sakura denbu*)), divided into 5 parts, each 25 g

1 small cheese sausage, 10-cm long

5 spinach stalks, each 10-cm long, blanched

1. Wrap the sausage with $1/3$ sheet of seaweed for the centre of the flower. Set aside.

2. Shape each 25 g of pink rice into a 10-cm rod and wrap with $1/3$ sheet of seaweed.

3. Arrange the wrapped sausage and rice rolls in the shape of a flower. Place a spinach stalk between each flower petal.

4. Wrap the flower roll with a thin strip of seaweed to keep it together. Set aside.

5. Spread 100 g white rice on the $1 1/3$ sheet of seaweed, leaving a 5-cm gap at one end.

6. Place the flower roll in the centre and start rolling up the roll.

7. Use the remaining white rice to fill any gaps before closing the roll.

8. Cut the roll into 4 pieces.

Plum Blossom 梅の木

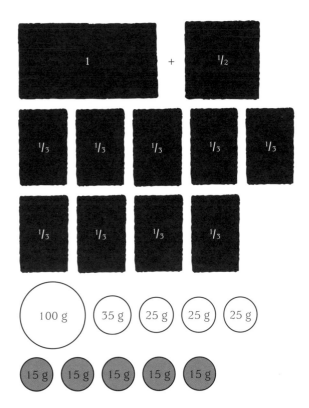

Ingredients

1 sheet + ¹/₂ sheet of seaweed, joined

9 x ¹/₃ sheet of seaweed

1 strip of seaweed, 10-cm x 1-cm

210 g white sushi rice, divided

75 g red sushi rice (65 g white sushi rice + 10 g fish roe powder (*mentaiko* powder)), divided into 5 parts, each 15 g

1 Chinese leek, 10-cm long, blanched

1 pickled gourd strip (*kanpyo*), 10-cm x 3-cm

1 tsp pink fish flakes (*oboro*) (page 29)

2 spinach stalks, each 10-cm long, blanched

1. Wrap the leek with ¹/₃ sheet of seaweed.

2. Shape each 15 g portion of red rice into a 10-cm cylinder and wrap with ¹/₃ sheet of seaweed.

3. Using a sushi mat, arrange the wrapped leek and rice rolls in the shape of a flower.

4. Bind the rolls together using a strip of seaweed. Set aside.

5. Wrap the pickled gourd with ¹/₃ sheet of seaweed for the flower stalk. Set aside.

6. Spread 100 g white rice on the 1¹/₂ sheet of seaweed, leaving a 5-cm gap at one end.

7. Place the flower roll in the centre.

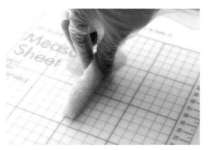

8. Shape three 10-cm long mountains, using 25 g white rice per mountain.

9. Arrange them side by side next to the flower roll.

10. Fold two ¹/₃ sheets of seaweed and place between the rice mountains.

11. Spoon the pink fish floss into the folded seaweed and top with a stalk of spinach. These are the buds.

12. Arrange the wrapped pickled gourd on the slope of the rice mountain at the side. Align it with the rice.

13. Roll up the sushi roll, making sure the valleys join and the wrapped pickled gourd touches the flower.

14. Use the remaining white rice to fill any gaps before closing the roll.

15. Cut the roll into 4 pieces.

Butterfly 蝶

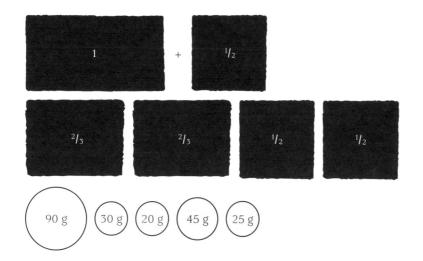

Ingredients

1 sheet + ¹/₂ sheet of seaweed, joined

2 x ²/₃ sheet of seaweed

2 x ¹/₂ sheet of seaweed

140 g white sushi rice, divided

70 g yellow sushi rice (approximately 60 g sushi rice + 1 hard-boiled egg yolk), divided

2 tsp pink fish floss (*sakura denbu*)

2 strips of Japanese cucumber, each 10-cm x 1-cm

1 fried tofu pocket (*aburaage*), cut to form a 10-cm x 4-cm piece

8 strips of ham for antennae

1. Spread 25 g yellow rice on ¹/₂ sheet of seaweed, leaving a 1-cm gap at one end and a 3-cm gap at the other end.

2. Spoon some pink fish floss in a line in the centre and top with a strip of cucumber.

3. Fold the roll up and press on one side to form a teardrop shape roll for the hindwing. Set aside.

4. Spread 45 g yellow rice on ²/₃ sheet of seaweed, leaving a 2-cm gap at one end. Top with pink fish floss and a strip of cucumber.

5. This time, roll the sushi up to create a spiral pattern for the forewing. Set aside.

6. Wrap the tofu pocket with ²/₃ sheet of seaweed for the body. Set aside

7. Spread 90 g white rice on the 1¹/₂ sheet of seaweed, leaving a 5-cm gap at each end.

8. Shape 20 g white rice into a 10-cm long mound and place in the centre.

9. Place the wrapped tofu pocket body over the mound.

10. Arrange the forewing and hindwing on the wrapped tofu pocket body.

11. Place the remaining rice around the sides for support and fill any gaps before closing the roll.

12. Cut the roll into 4 pieces. Finish with ham antennae.

Bee 蜂

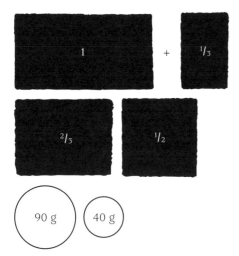

Ingredients

1 sheet + ¹/₃ sheet of seaweed, joined

1 x ²/₃ sheet of seaweed

1 x ¹/₂ sheet of seaweed

130 g white sushi rice, divided

1 grilled omelette (*tamagoyaki*), 10-cm x 4-cm (page 30)

2 pickled gourd strips (*kanpyo*), each 10-cm x 3-cm

4 circles of seaweed for eyes

4 circles of ham for cheeks

1. Cut the grilled omelette lengthwise into 3 parts for the body.

2. Trim the pickled gourd strips to the size of the grilled omelette. Place a strip between each piece of omelette.

3. Wrap the grilled omelette with $^2/_3$ sheet of seaweed. Set aside.

4. Shape 30 g white rice into a 10-cm oblong on $^1/_2$ sheet of seaweed. Roll up.

5. Cut the oblong lengthwise in half for the wings. Set aside.

6. Spread 90 g white rice on the $1^1/_2$ sheet of seaweed, leaving a 6-cm gap at one end.

7. Place the wrapped grilled omelette in the centre, followed by the wings, cut-side down.

8. Use the remaining white rice to fill any gaps before closing the roll.

9. Cut the roll into 4 pieces. Finish with a seaweed eye and ham cheek.

Sakura Flower 桜

Ingredients

$^2/_3$ sheet of seaweed

1 strip of seaweed, 10-cm x 1$^1/_2$-cm

45 g pink sushi rice (35 g white sushi rice + 10 g pink fish flakes (*oboro*) (page 29))

NOTE This recipe yields only 1 sakura flower.

1. Spread 45 g of pink rice on $^2/_3$ sheet of seaweed, leaving a 2-cm gap at one end.

2. Place a strip of seaweed on the edge of the rice.

3. Fold the roll up tightly.

4. Press on one side to form a teardrop shape roll.

5. Use a chopstick to press down on the wider end of the roll to create a ridge.

6. Cut the roll into 5 pieces and arrange in the shape of a flower.

Autumn Themed Sushi

Maple Leaf 50

Chestnut 54

Mushroom 56

Maple Leaf 紅葉

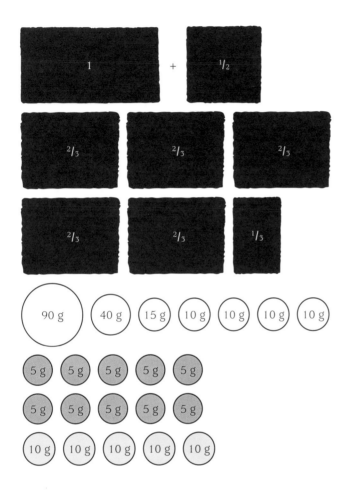

Ingredients

1 sheet + $^1/_2$ sheet of seaweed, joined

5 x $^2/_3$ sheet of seaweed

1 x $^1/_3$ sheet of seaweed

185 g white sushi rice, divided

50 g orange sushi rice (42 g white sushi rice + 8 g flying fish roe (*tobiko*)), divided into 10 parts, each 5 g

50 g yellow sushi rice (approximately 50 g white sushi rice + 1 hard-boiled egg yolk), divided into 5 parts, each 10 g

2 pickled gourd strips (*kanpyo*), each 10-cm x 3-cm

1. Spread 2 parts orange rice and 1 part yellow rice alternately on $^2/_3$ sheet of seaweed, leaving a 2-cm gap at one end.

2. Fold the roll up tightly and press on the orange rice to form a teardrop shape roll. Repeat to make another 4 rolls.

3. Twist a pickled gourd strip tightly for the end of the leaf stem. Set aside.

4. Wrap the other pickled gourd strip with $^1/_3$ sheet of seaweed for the leaf stem. Set aside.

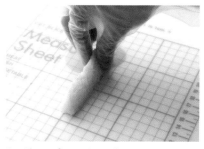

5. Shape four 10-cm long mountains, using 10 g white rice per mountain.

6. Spread 90 g white rice on the $1^1/_2$ sheet of seaweed, leaving a 5-cm gap at one end.

7. Alternate 3 parts of the leaf with 2 rice mountains.

8. Place them in the centre of the rice.

9. Continue to build up the leaf with the remaining rice mountains and parts of the leaf.

10. Adjust the position of the rolls if needed to form the shape of the maple leaf.

11. Place the twisted pickled gourd strip in the centre of the leaf.

12. Place the wrapped pickled gourd strip on top of the twisted pickled gourd strip.

13. Top with 40 g white rice. Use the remaining white rice to fill any gaps before closing the roll.

14. Cut the roll into 4 pieces.

Chestnut 栗

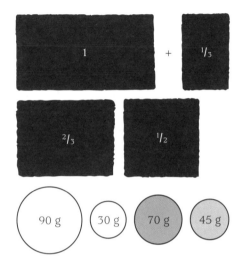

Ingredients

1 sheet + $^1/_3$ sheet of seaweed, joined

1 x $^1/_2$ sheet of seaweed

1 x $^2/_3$ sheet of seaweed

120 g white sushi rice, divided

70 g dark brown sushi rice (60 g white sushi rice + 10 g bonito flakes soft rice topping (*okaka* soft *furikake*))

45 g brown sushi rice (40 g white sushi rice + 5 g roasted sesame and teriyaki sauce)

Roasted white sesame seeds

1. Shape 45 g brown rice into a 10-cm oval and wrap with $^1/_2$ sheet of seaweed.

2. Using the sushi mat, shape it into an oval for the base of the chestnut.

3. Shape 70 g dark brown rice into a 10-cm mountain for the top of the chestnut.

4. Place the roll from step 1 on a $^2/_3$ sheet of seaweed, then place the mountain from step 3 on it.

5. Close the roll up and shape to resemble a chestnut.

6. Spread 90 g white rice on the $1\,^1/_3$ sheet of seaweed, leaving a 6-cm gap at one end.

7. Place the chestnut roll in the centre. Sprinkle sesame seeds on the rice.

8. Start rolling up the roll. Use the remaining white rice to fill any gaps before closing the roll.

9. Cut the roll into 4 pieces.

Mushroom キノコ

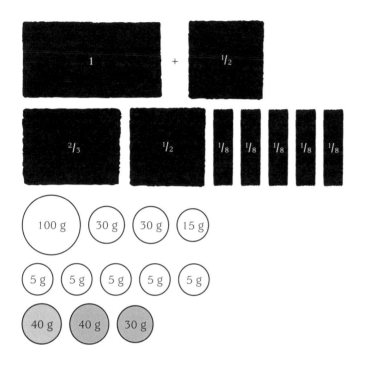

Ingredients

1 sheet + ¹/₂ sheet of seaweed, joined

1 x ²/₃ sheet of seaweed

1 x ¹/₂ sheet of seaweed

5 x ¹/₈ sheet of seaweed

200 g white sushi rice, divided

70 g orange sushi rice (62 g white sushi rice + 8 g fish roe powder (*mentaiko* powder)), divided

40 g light brown sushi rice (35 g white sushi rice + 5 g roasted soy bean rice topping (*kinako furikake*))

1. Prepare 5 portions of white rice each weighing 5 g. Shape each portion into a 10-cm rod and wrap each rod with $^1/_8$ sheet of seaweed.

2. Spread 30 g orange rice on $^2/_3$ sheet of seaweed, leaving a 5-cm gap at both ends.

3. Arrange 3 rods slightly apart on the orange rice.

4. Fill the gaps between the rods with orange rice.

5. Place the remaining 2 white rods on the orange rice.

6. Repeat to fill the gap between the rods with orange rice.

7. Use the remaining orange rice to cover the rods completely.

8. Close up the roll and shape to resemble a mushroom cap.

9. Shape 40 g light brown rice into a 10-cm oblong and place on $^1/_2$ sheet of seaweed.

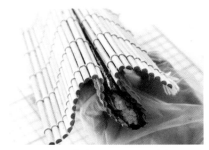

10. Wrap and shape into an oblong roll for the mushroom stem.

11. Slice a thin strip from one side of the roll and discard.

12. Spread 100 g white rice on the $1^1/_2$ sheet of seaweed, leaving a 6-cm gap at one end.

13. Place the mushroom cap in the centre, concave side up. Place the stem, cut-side down on the cap.

14. Spread 30 g white rice on each side of the stem.

15. Start rolling up the roll. Use the remaining white rice to fill any gaps before closing the roll.

16. Cut the roll into 4 pieces.

Food Themed Sushi

Watermelon スイカ

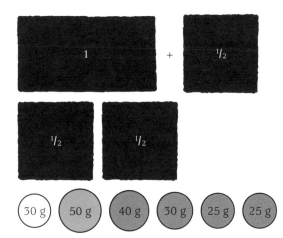

Ingredients

1 sheet + 1/2 sheet of seaweed, joined

2 x 1/2 sheet of seaweed

30 g white sushi rice

50 g green sushi rice (40 g white sushi rice + 10 g chopped marinated seaweed (*chuka wakame*))

120 g red sushi rice (100 g white sushi rice + 20 g pink fish flakes (*oboro*) (page 29)), divided

2 pickled gourd strips (*kanpyo*), 10-cm x 2-cm, each cut lengthwise into 3 strips

1. Spread 50 g green rice in the centre of the 1½ sheet of seaweed, shaping it 6-cm wide for the rind.

2. Place ½ sheet of seaweed over the green rice and fold down the sides.

3. Spread with 30 g white rice, shaping it 5-cm wide for the white flesh. Cover with ½ sheet of seaweed.

4. Repeat to spread 40 g red rice on the seaweed, shaping it 4-cm wide for the red flesh.

5. Use a skewer to make 3 indents, then place a pickled gourd strip into each indent for the seeds.

6. Top with 30 g red rice, then make 2 indents for another 2 pickled gourd strips.

7. Top with 25 g red rice, followed by the last pickled gourd strip.

8. Cover with 25 g red rice, shaping it with a pointed top to resemble a wedge of watermelon.

9. Close up the roll, shaping in into a triangular shape.

10. Cut the roll into 4 pieces.

Cherries さくらんぼ

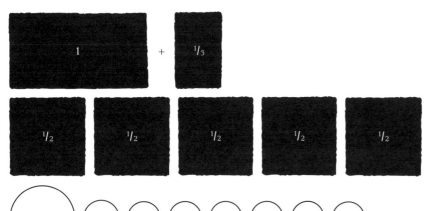

Ingredients

1 sheet + $^1/_3$ sheet of seaweed, joined

5 x $^1/_2$ sheet of seaweed

230 g white sushi rice, divided

1 pickled gourd strip (*kanpyo*), 10-cm x 3-cm

2 small meat sausages, each 10-cm long

1. Wrap the pickled gourd with ½ sheet of seaweed for the big stem. Set aside.

2. Spread 90 g white rice on the 1⅓ sheet of seaweed, leaving a 6-cm gap at one end.

3. Shape three 10-cm long mountains, using 20 g white rice per mountain. Arrange them in the centre.

4. Fold two ½ sheets of seaweed and place them in the valley between the mountains.

5. Place a sausage in each folded seaweed for the cherries, then slot in another two ½ sheets of seaweed on top of the sausages.

6. Close the seaweed with 20 g white rice on both sides.

7. Top with the wrapped pickled gourd.

8. Cover the pickled gourd with 30 g white rice. Use the remaining rice to fill any gaps before closing the roll.

9. Cut the roll into 4 pieces.

Bananas バナナ

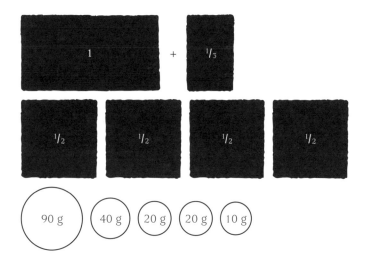

Ingredients

1 sheet + ¹/₃ sheet of seaweed, joined

4 x ¹/₂ sheet of seaweed

180 g white sushi rice, divided

3 mini grilled omelettes (*tamagoyaki*), 10-cm x 3.5-cm (page 30)

¹/₂ Japanese cucumber, 10-cm long

1. Wrap the grilled omelettes individually with $^1/_2$ sheet of seaweed for the bananas.

2. Wrap the cucumber with $^1/_2$ sheet of seaweed for the stem.

3. Spread 90 g white rice on the 1$^1/_3$ sheet of seaweed, leaving a 5-cm gap at one end.

4. Place the wrapped cucumber, flat-side down on the rice.

5. Position the 3 wrapped omelettes on top of the cucumber.

6. Hold the omelettes in place with 20 g white rice on each side.

7. Fill the gaps between the omelettes with 10 g white rice.

8. Start rolling up the roll. Use the 40 g white rice to fill any gaps before closing the roll.

9. Cut the roll into 4 pieces.

Lemon レモン

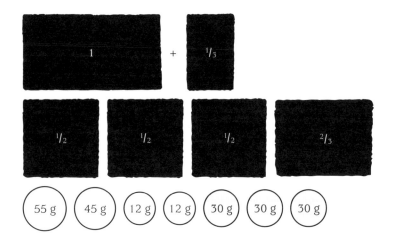

1 + 1/3

1/2   1/2   1/2   2/3

55 g   45 g   12 g   12 g   30 g   30 g   30 g

Ingredients

1 sheet + 1/3 sheet of seaweed, joined

3 x 1/2 sheet of seaweed

1 x 2/3 sheet of seaweed

125 g white sushi rice, divided

90 g yellow sushi rice (approximately 75 g white sushi rice + 1 hard-boiled egg yolk), divided into 3 parts, each 30 g

1 large egg sheet (page 31)

Roasted white sesame seeds

1. Shape each portion of yellow rice into an equilateral triangle with 2-cm sides. Make each 10-cm long.

2. Wrap each yellow rice triangle with $^1/_3$ sheet of seaweed. Set aside.

3. Shape 12 g white rice into a 10-cm x 2-cm strip. Repeat to make another strip. Set aside.

4. Alternate the yellow rice triangles with the white rice strips, packing them closely together. Set aside.

5. Spread 45 g white rice in the centre of the $1^1/_3$ sheet of seaweed, shaping it 6-cm wide.

6. Place the roll from step 4 on the rice.

7. Spread 55 g white rice thinly over the roll.

8. Place $^2/_3$ sheet of seaweed over the white rice and fold down the sides.

9. Place the egg sheet over the seaweed. Trim the edges if necessary.

10. Roll up the roll. Seal the seaweed with a few grains of sushi rice if needed.

11. Cut the roll into 4 pieces. Finish with roasted white sesame seeds for the seeds of the lemon.

Candy キャンディ

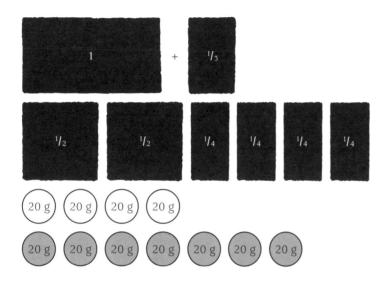

Ingredients

1 sheet + $^1/_3$ sheet of seaweed, joined

2 x $^1/_2$ sheet of seaweed

4 x $^1/_4$ sheet of seaweed

80 g white sushi rice, divided into 4 parts, each 20 g

140 g purple sushi rice (140 g white sushi rice + 2 g dehydrated purple sweet potato powder), divided into 7 parts, each 20 g

1. Spread 3 purple and 2 white parts of rice on the 1$\frac{1}{3}$ sheet of seaweed. Shape each 3.5-cm wide, leaving a 3-cm gap at the end.

2. Roll the sushi up to create a spiral pattern. Cut into 4 pieces. Set aside.

3. Shape remaining portions of rice into 10-cm mountains for the sweet wrapper.

4. Arrange 2 purple and 1 white mountain on $\frac{1}{2}$ sheet of seaweed.

5. Fold two $\frac{1}{4}$ sheets of seaweed and place them in the valley between the mountains.

6. Trim the excess seaweed with a pair of scissors.

7. Repeat steps 4–6 to make another set. Cut each set into 4 pieces.

8. Assemble the parts to complete the candy.

Animal Themed Sushi

Panda パンダさん

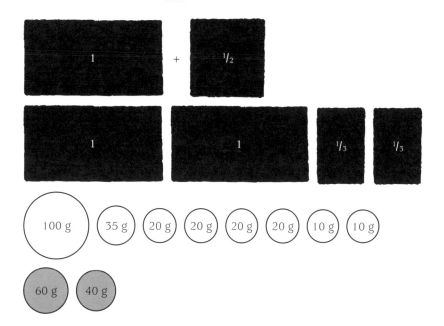

Ingredients

1 sheet + ¹/₂ sheet of seaweed, joined

2 sheets of seaweed

2 x ¹/₃ sheet of seaweed

235 g white sushi rice, divided

100 g black sushi rice (95 g white sushi rice + 5 g ground black sesame (*suri goma*)), divided

2 pickled gourd strips (*kanpyo*), each 10-cm x 2-cm

8 circles of seaweed for eyes

1. Pat dry pickled gourd strips and wrap each one separately with ¹/₃ sheet of seaweed. Set one aside for the mouth.

2. Roll the other wrapped pickled gourd strip up tightly for the nose. Set aside.

3. Shape 40 g black rice into a 20-cm long rod and align it on the long side of 1 sheet of seaweed.

4. Roll the rod up tightly and trim away any excess seaweed.

5. Divide the roll into 8 parts for the ears. Set aside.

6. Shape 60 g black rice into a 20-cm long rod and align it on the long side of 1 sheet of seaweed.

7. Roll the rod up tightly into an oval roll. Trim away any excess seaweed.

8. Cut the roll in half for the eyes. Set aside.

9. Spread 100 g white rice on the 1¹/₂ sheet of seaweed, leaving a 5-cm gap at each end.

10. Shape 20 g white rice into a 10-cm long mound and place in the centre.

11. Shape another 20 g white rice into a 10-cm strip and place it on the mound.

12. Place a black rice roll on each side of the mound of white rice for the eyes.

13. Place the rolled up pickled gourd strip in the centre of the mound of white rice for the nose.

14. Top each eye with 20 g white rice to build up the panda's face.

15. Using a sushi mat, gently shape the wrapped pickled gourd strip into a V for the mouth. Fill with 10 g white rice to secure the shape.

16. Place the mouth on the nose, then top with 35 g white rice, shaping it into a dome.

17. Start rolling up the roll. Use the remaining white rice to fill any gaps before closing the roll.

18. Cut the roll into 4 pieces. Assemble the ears and finish with seaweed eyes.

Hen めんどりさん

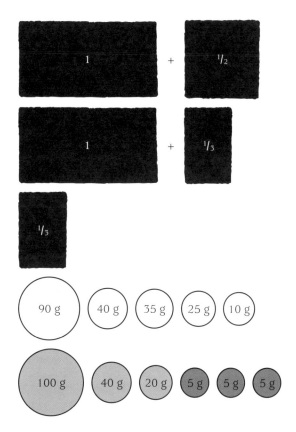

Ingredients

1 sheet + ¹/₂ sheet of seaweed, joined

1 sheet + ¹/₃ sheet of seaweed, joined

1 x ¹/₃ sheet of seaweed

175 g white sushi rice, divided

160 g pink sushi rice (125 g white sushi rice + 35 g pink fish flakes (*oboro*) (page 29)), divided

15 g red sushi rice (10 g white sushi rice + 5 g fish roe powder (*mentaiko* powder)), divided into 3 parts, each 5 g

4 circles of seaweed for eyes

4 triangular pieces of egg sheet (page 31) for beaks

1. Shape 25 g white rice into a 10-cm long oval and wrap with $^1/_3$ sheet of seaweed for the wing.

2. Line a bamboo mat with cling wrap and place the wing on the mat.

3. Shape 90 g white rice into a 10-cm long curved shape and place it over the wing.

4. Cover with cling wrap and use the sushi mat to shape the rice for the body.

5. Unwrap the roll and place it in the centre of the $1^1/_3$ sheet of seaweed.

6. Top with 40 g white rice and cover the wing.

7. Shape 10 g white rice into a 10-cm long mountain and place it on one end of the body for the tail.

8. Shape 35 g white rice into a 10-cm long oval and place it on the other end of the body for the head.

9. Close up the roll, using the sushi mat to shape the roll and press the seaweed into the grooves.

10. Spread 100 g pink rice on the 1¹/₂ sheet of seaweed, leaving a 5-cm gap at each end.

11. Place the roll for the hen's body in the centre.

12. Shape 5 g red rice into a 10-cm long mountain. Make another 2 and place on the head for the comb.

13. Place a ¹/₃ sheet of seaweed over the comb, folding it into the grooves.

14. Top the back of the hen with 20 g pink rice to fill up the gap.

15. Start rolling up the roll. Top the comb with some pink rice and fill any gaps with the remaining pink rice before closing the roll.

16. Cut the roll into 4 pieces. Finish with a seaweed eye and sliced egg sheet beak.

Bunny うさぎちゃん

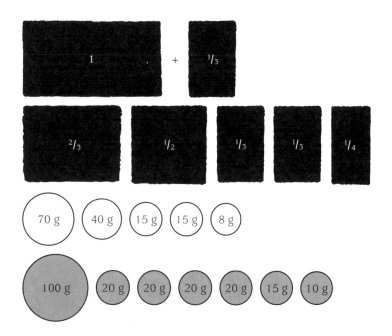

Ingredients

1 sheet + ⅓ sheet of seaweed, joined

1 x ⅔ sheet of seaweed

1 x ½ sheet of seaweed

2 x ⅓ sheet of seaweed

1 x ¼ sheet of seaweed

148 g white sushi rice, divided

205 g pink sushi rice (150 g white sushi rice + 55 g pink fish flakes (*oboro*) (page 29)), divided

4 circles of seaweed for eyes

1. Shape 70 g white rice into a 10-cm long curved shape and wrap with ²/₃ sheet seaweed for the body.

2. Use the sushi mat to enhance the shape of the curve. Set aside.

3. Shape 40 g white rice into a 10-cm long roll and wrap with ¹/₂ sheet seaweed for the head. Set aside.

4. Shape 8 g white rice into a 10-cm long rod and wrap with ¹/₄ seaweed for the tail. Set aside.

5. Spread 15 g white rice on ¹/₃ sheet seaweed, leaving a 1-cm gap on both sides.

6. Fold the roll up tightly. Press on one side to form a teardrop shape roll for the ear.

7. Repeat to make another teardrop shape roll for the other ear. Trim away the excess seaweed.

8. Spread 100 g pink rice on the 1¹/₃ sheet of seaweed, leaving a 5-cm gap at each end.

9. Shape 20 g pink rice into a 10-cm long mound and place it in the centre.

10. Place the body on the mound, concave side down. Place the head at one end and the tail at the other. (See step 11)

11. Fill the gap below the head with 20 g pink rice and the gap between the head and tail with another 10 g pink rice.

12. Press the rolls for the ears together and place them, pointed side down on the head.

13. Fill the gaps between the ears and head with 15 g pink rice, and the ears and tail with 20 g pink rice.

14. Start rolling up the roll. Use the remaining pink rice to fill any gaps before closing the roll.

15. Cut the roll into 4 pieces. Finish with seaweed eyes.

Sheep 羊さん

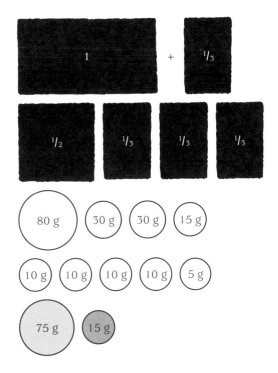

Ingredients

1 sheet + ¹/₃ sheet of seaweed, joined

1 x ¹/₂ sheet of seaweed

3 x ¹/₃ sheet of seaweed

4 strips of seaweed, each 10-cm x 1-cm

200 g sushi rice, divided

75 g light brown sushi rice (75 g white sushi rice + teriyaki sauce)

15 g black sushi rice (12 g white sushi rice + 3 g ground black sesame (*suri goma*))

4 fried tofu pockets (*aburaage*)

8 curved lines of seaweed for eyes

1. Shape 15 g black rice into a 10-cm long flat oval and wrap with ¹/₃ sheet seaweed.

2. Cut lengthwise in half, then cut into 4 pieces each for the legs. Set aside.

3. Shape 10 g white rice into a rod and wrap with ¹/₃ sheet seaweed. Repeat to make 2 rolls.

4. Cut each roll lengthwise in half for the poll of the sheep.

5. Align 2 halves, cut-side up. Spread 15 g white rice in the centre of the cut rolls.

6. Place the remaining 2 halves, cut-side down, on the rice.

7. Fold the 10-cm x 1-cm strips of seaweed lengthwise in half. Place a strip between each half-roll. Set aside.

8. Using a lined sushi mat, compact 30 g light brown rice into a 10-cm long oval for the head.

9. Place ¹/₂ sheet seaweed over the roll. Do not cover the rice roll fully as shown in picture. Set aside.

10. Cut the tofu pockets to form two 10-cm x 6-cm pieces for the sheep's horns.

11. On a lined sushi mat, roll each tofu pocket up tightly. Wrap with cling wrap and set aside.

12. Spread 80 g white rice on the $1\frac{1}{3}$ sheet of seaweed, leaving a 5-cm gap at each end.

13. Place the poll in the centre, then spread 10 g white rice on each side.

14. Place the head on the poll, with the exposed side facing down.

15. Peel off the cling wrap and arrange the horns on each side of the head.

16. Secure in position using 30 g white rice on each side, shaping it into a dome.

17. Start rolling up the roll. Use the remaining white rice to fill any gaps before closing the roll.

18. Cut the roll into 4 pieces. Assemble the legs and finish with seaweed eyes.

Chick ひよこちゃん

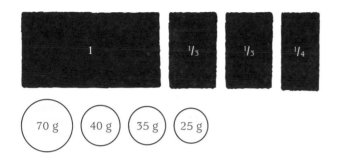

| 1 | ¹/₃ | ¹/₃ | ¹/₄ |

| 70 g | 40 g | 35 g | 25 g |

Ingredients

1 sheet of seaweed

2 x ¹/₃ sheet of seaweed

1 x ¹/₄ sheet of seaweed

170 g yellow sushi rice
(approximately 150 g white sushi
rice + 2 hard-boiled egg yolks),
divided

1 pickled burdock (*yamagobo*),
10-cm long

2 pickled gourd strips (*kanpyo*),
each 10-cm x 2-cm

1. Pat dry burdock and wrap tightly with ¹/₄ sheet seaweed for the beak. Set aside.

2. Pat dry pickled gourd strips and wrap separately with ¹/₃ sheet of seaweed. Roll each one up tightly for the eyes. Set aside.

3. Spread 70 g yellow rice on 1 sheet of seaweed, leaving a 4-cm gap at each end.

4. Shape 25 g yellow rice into a 10-cm long mound and place in the centre.

5. Position a rolled up pickled gourd strip on each side of the mound for the eyes.

6. Place the rolled up burdock on top of the mound for the beak.

7. Top with 40 g yellow rice to hold the beak and eyes in place. Shape it into a dome.

8. Start rolling up the roll. Use the remaining yellow rice to fill any gaps before closing the roll.

9. Cut the roll into 4 pieces. Finish with a heart shape bento pick for the comb.

Bear くまさん

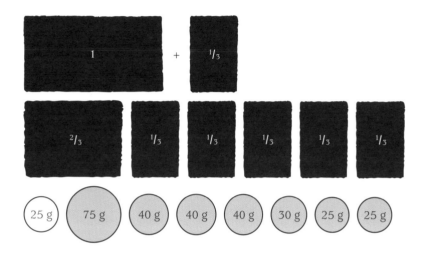

Ingredients

1 sheet + $^1/_3$ sheet of seaweed, joined

1 x $^2/_3$ sheet of seaweed

5 x $^1/_3$ sheet of seaweed

25 g white sushi rice

275 g brown sushi rice (250 g white sushi rice + 25 g bonito flakes soft rice topping (*okaka* soft *furikake*)), divided

2 pickled gourd strips (*kanpyo*), each 10-cm x 2-cm

1 small cheese sausage, 10-cm long

4 circles + 4 short strips of seaweed for noses

1. Pat dry pickled gourd strips and wrap separately with ¹/₃ sheet of seaweed. Roll each one up tightly for the eyes. Set aside.

2. Shape 25 g white rice into a 10-cm rod and wrap with ¹/₃ sheet of seaweed. Roll up tightly for the muzzle. Set aside.

3. Spread 40 g brown rice on ²/₃ sheet of seaweed, leaving a 5-cm gap at one end.

4. Place a sausage on the rice and roll up tightly for the ears.

5. Cut the roll lengthwise in half, then cut into 4 pieces each. Set aside.

6. Shape 75 g brown rice into a 10-cm long mountain and place in the centre of the 1¹/₃ sheet of seaweed.

7. Place a ¹/₃ sheet of seaweed on each side of the mountain.

8. Spread 40 g brown rice on each side of the mountain.

9. Place a pickled gourd strip eye on each mound of brown rice and the muzzle in the centre.

10. Top both sides with 25 g brown rice to hold the parts in place. Start rolling up the roll.

11. Use 30 g brown rice to cover the muzzle, filling any gaps and forming the shape of the head before closing the roll.

12. Cut the roll into 4 pieces. Assemble the ears and finish with a seaweed nose.

Puppy 犬さん

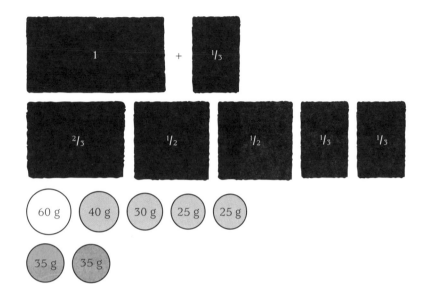

1 + 1/3

2/3 | 1/2 | 1/2 | 1/3 | 1/3

60 g | 40 g | 30 g | 25 g | 25 g

35 g | 35 g

Ingredients

1 sheet + 1/3 sheet of seaweed, joined

1 x 2/3 sheet of seaweed

2 x 1/2 sheet of seaweed

2 x 1/3 sheet of seaweed

60 g white sushi rice

120 g light brown sushi rice (120 g white sushi rice + teriyaki sauce), divided

70 g black sushi rice (60 g white sushi rice + 10 g ground black sesame (*suri goma*)), divided

2 pickled gourd strips (*kanpyo*), each 10-cm x 2-cm

4 ovals of seaweed for noses

4 U-shaped pieces of ham for tongues

1. Pat dry pickled gourd strips and wrap separately with ⅓ sheet of seaweed.

2. Roll each one up tightly for the eyes. Set aside.

3. Shape 35 g black rice into a 10-cm long oval and wrap with ½ sheet of seaweed for the ears.

4. Repeat to make another roll. Trim away any excess seaweed. Set aside.

5. Shape 60 g white rice into a 10-cm long mound and wrap with ⅔ sheet of seaweed for the muzzle.

6. Place in the centre of the 1⅓ sheet of seaweed.

7. Spread 25 g light brown rice on each side of the mound.

8. Place a pickled gourd strip eye on each mound of light brown rice.

9. Top with 40 g light brown rice to hold the parts in place and form the shape of the head.

10. Place the ears above the eyes.

11. Fill the gaps between the ears with 30 g light brown rice and close the roll.

12. Cut the roll into 4 pieces. Finish with a seaweed nose and ham tongue.

Transport Themed Sushi

Train Engine 列車

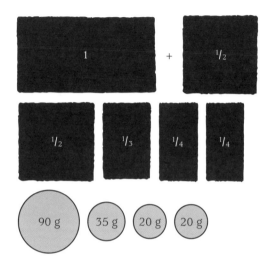

Ingredients

1 sheet + ¹/₂ sheet of seaweed, joined

1 x ¹/₂ sheet seaweed

1 x ¹/₃ sheet seaweed

2 x ¹/₄ sheet of seaweed

165 g pink sushi rice (130 g white sushi rice + 35 g pink fish flakes (*oboro*) (page 29)), divided

2 pickled burdock (*yamagobo*), 10-cm long

1 grilled omelette (*tamagoyaki*), 10-cm x 3-cm x 1.5-cm (page 30)

1 Japanese fish roll (*kamaboko*), pink part 10-cm x 2-cm x 0.5-cm and white part 10-cm x 1.5-cm x 1-cm

4 small strips of seaweed for the chimney

1. Pat dry burdock and wrap each one tightly with ¹/₄ sheet of seaweed for the wheels. Set aside.

2. Wrap the grilled omelette with ¹/₂ sheet of seaweed for the engine. Set aside.

3. Wrap the white fish roll with ¹/₃ sheet of seaweed for the cabin. Set aside.

4. Spread 90 g pink rice on the 1¹/₂ sheet of seaweed, leaving a 5-cm gap at each end.

5. Place the pink fish roll slightly off centre on the rice for the roof of the cabin.

6. Place the wrapped white fish roll on it, aligning it to the right.

7. Spread 20 g pink rice on the left of the fish roll.

8. Place the grilled omelette on the white fish roll, again aligning it to the right.

9. Place the wrapped burdock wheels on the grilled omelette, spacing them slightly apart.

10. Top with 35 g pink rice to hold the wheels in place.

11. Start rolling up the roll. Use the remaining pink rice to fill any gaps before closing the roll.

12. Cut the roll into 4 pieces. Finish with a seaweed chimney.

Train Carriage 客車

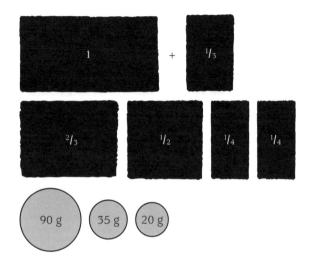

Ingredients

1 sheet + ⅓ sheet of seaweed, joined

1 x ⅔ sheet seaweed

1 x ½ sheet seaweed

2 x ¼ sheet of seaweed

2 strips of seaweed, each 10-cm x 1-cm

145 g pink sushi rice (115 g white sushi rice + 30 g pink fish flakes (*oboro*) (page 29)), divided

2 pickled burdock (*yamagobo*), 10-cm long

1 grilled omelette (*tamagoyaki*), 10-cm x 3-cm x 1.5-cm (page 30)

1 Japanese fish roll (*kamaboko*), white part, 10-cm x 3-cm x 1-cm

1. Pat dry burdock and wrap each one tightly with ¹/₄ sheet of seaweed for the wheels. Set aside.

2. Wrap the grilled omelette with ¹/₂ sheet of seaweed for the cabin. Set aside.

3. Cut the fish roll lengthwise to get 3 equal pieces for the windows of the cabin.

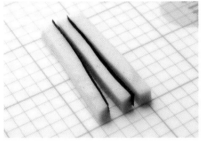

4. Place a strip of seaweed between the pieces of fish roll.

5. Wrap the fish roll with ²/₃ sheet of seaweed. Set aside.

6. Spread 90 g pink rice on the 1 ¹/₃ sheet of seaweed, leaving a 5-cm gap at each end.

7. Place the wrapped fish roll in the centre.

8. Place the wrapped grilled omelette on the fish roll.

9. Place the wrapped burdock wheels on the grilled omelette, spacing them slightly apart.

10. Top with 35 g pink rice to hold the wheels in place.

11. Start rolling up the roll. Use the remaining pink rice to fill any gaps before closing the roll.

12. Cut the roll into 4 pieces. Complete the train with the engine (page 98).

Police Car パトカー

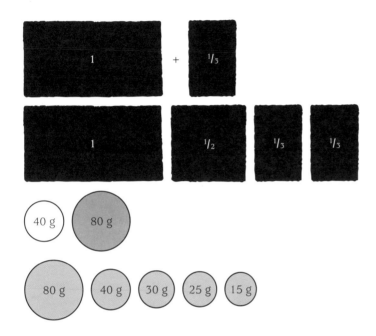

Ingredients

1 sheet + $^1/_3$ sheet of seaweed, joined

1 sheet of seaweed

1 x $^1/_2$ seaweed

2 x $^1/_3$ sheet of seaweed

1 strip of seaweed, 10-cm x 2-cm

40 g white sushi rice

80 g black sushi rice (70 g white sushi rice + 10 g ground black sesame (*suri goma*))

190 g pink sushi rice (155 g white sushi rice + 35 g pink fish flakes (*oboro*) (page 29)), divided

2 small cheese sausages, 10-cm long

1 halved Japanese cucumber, 10-cm long

1 pickled burdock (*yamagobo*), 10-cm long

NOTE Turn this into a regular car by using rice in a single colour and omitting the pickled burdock siren on the roof.

1. Wrap the sausages individually with $^1/_3$ sheet of seaweed for the wheels. Set aside.

2. Cut the cucumber in half and place the strip of seaweed in the middle.

3. Wrap it with $^1/_2$ sheet of seaweed for the windows. Set aside.

4. Cut the pickled burdock lengthwise in half. Set one strip aside for another use.

5. Compact 80 g black sushi rice into a 10-cm x 6-cm block. Place on 1 sheet of seaweed.

6. Place the wrapped cucumber windows slightly off centre on the rice.

7. Top with 40 g white rice, shaping it into a dome for the roof. Wrap with the seaweed and set aside.

8. Spread 80 g pink rice on the $1^1/_3$ sheet of seaweed, leaving a 5-cm gap at each end. Set aside.

9. Spread 30 g pink rice on the larger gap at the side of the car and 15 g pink rice on the other side.

10. Place half a strip of burdock on the roof for the siren.

11. Invert the roll on the rice, being careful to keep the siren in place.

12. Place the wrapped sausage wheels on the roll, spacing them slightly apart.

13. Top with 40 g pink rice to hold the wheels in place.

14. Start rolling up the roll. Use the remaining pink rice to fill any gaps before closing the roll.

15. Cut the roll into 4 pieces.

Sailing Boat セーリングボート

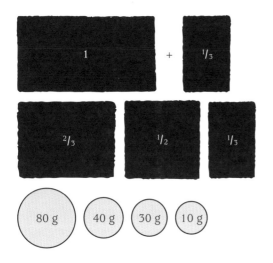

Ingredients

1 sheet + $^1/_3$ sheet of seaweed, joined

1 x $^2/_3$ sheet seaweed

1 x $^1/_2$ sheet of seaweed

1 x $^1/_3$ sheet of seaweed

160 g light green sushi rice (135 g white sushi rice + 25 g marinated seaweed (*chuka wakame*)), divided

1 mini grilled omelette (*tamagoyaki*), 10-cm x 3.5-cm (page 30)

1 Japanese fish roll (*kamaboko*), 10-cm long

1 pickled gourd strip (*kanpyo*), 10-cm x 3-cm

1. Trim the grilled omelette to form the hull of the sailing boat.

2. Wrap the grilled omelette with ²/₃ sheet of seaweed. Set aside.

3. Cut the fish roll in half for the sail. Set the other half aside for use in another recipe.

4. Wrap the fish roll with ¹/₂ sheet of seaweed. Set aside.

5. Pat dry the pickled gourd strip and wrap with ¹/₃ sheet of seaweed for the mast. Set aside.

6. Spread 80 g green rice on the 1¹/₃ sheet of seaweed, leaving a 5-cm gap at each end.

7. Place the wrapped grilled omelette in the centre.

8. Spread 10 g green rice on one side of the grilled omelette.

9. Place the wrapped fish roll on the rice and the wrapped pickled gourd strip on the flat-side of the fish roll.

10. Spread 40 g green rice on the wrapped pickled gourd strip to fill the gap.

11. Start rolling up the roll. Use the remaining green rice to fill any gaps before closing the roll.

12. Cut the roll into 4 pieces.

Truck トラック

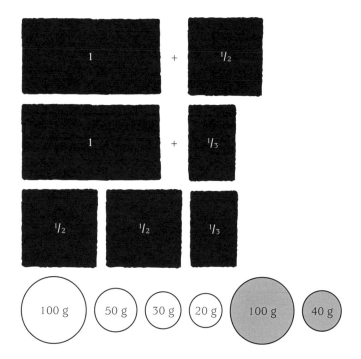

Ingredients

- 1 sheet + ½ sheet of seaweed, joined
- 1 sheet + ⅓ sheet of seaweed, joined
- 2 x ½ sheet of seaweed
- 1 x ⅓ sheet of seaweed
- 200 g white sushi rice, divided
- 140 g orange sushi rice (115 g white sushi rice + 25 g prawn roe (*ebiko*)), divided
- 1 small fish sausage, 10-cm long
- ¼ Japanese cucumber, 10-cm long
- 4 small pieces of sliced cheese for headlights
- 8 long + 16 short strips of seaweed for ladders

1. Cut the sausage in half lengthwise and wrap each half with $^1/_2$ sheet of seaweed for the wheels. Set aside.

2. Wrap the cucumber with $^1/_3$ sheet of seaweed for the window. Set aside.

3. Compact 100 g orange rice into a 10-cm x 6-cm block. Place in the centre of the $1^1/_3$ sheet of seaweed.

4. Place the wrapped cucumber to one side of the rice, curved side out, for the window.

5. Spread 40 g orange rice over the wrapped cucumber for the cabin.

6. Close up the roll, using the sushi mat to shape the roll and press the seaweed into the grooves.

7. Spread 50 g white rice on the side of the truck. Set aside.

8. Spread 100 g white rice on the $1^1/_2$ sheet of seaweed, leaving a 5-cm gap at each end.

9. Invert the roll on the rice and place the wrapped sausage halves on the roll, spacing them slightly apart.

10. Top with 30 g white rice to hold the wheels in place.

11. Start rolling up the roll. Use the remaining white rice to fill any gaps before closing the roll.

12. Cut the roll into 4 pieces. Finish with sliced cheese headlights and seaweed ladder.

Romance Themed Sushi

Rose バラ

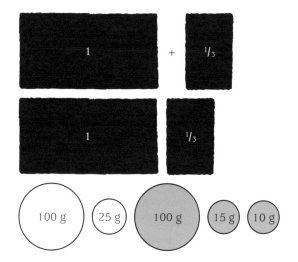

Ingredients

1 sheet + $^1/_3$ sheet of seaweed, joined

1 x $^1/_3$ sheet of seaweed

1 sheet of seaweed

125 g white sushi rice, divided

125 g red sushi rice (105 g white sushi rice + 20 g chopped red ginger), divided

1 Japanese cucumber, 10-cm long

1. Spread 15 g red rice on ¹/₃ sheet of seaweed, leaving a 1-cm gap at one end.

2. Roll the sushi up to create a spiral pattern for the centre of the rose. Set aside.

3. Line a sushi mat with cling wrap and shape 100 g red rice into a 20-cm long mound. Cut the mound into 2 equal pieces.

4. Place the 2 halves flat-side up on 1 sheet of seaweed.

5. Using a sushi mat, fold the seaweed over the 2 halves.

6. Spread 10 g red rice in the gap between the 2 halves.

7. Place the roll from step 2 on the rice to complete the rose. Set aside.

8. Spread 100 g white rice on the 1¹/₃ sheet of seaweed, leaving a 5-cm gap at each end.

9. Cut the cucumber lengthwise in half and place in the centre, flat-side up.

10. Place the rose roll between the cucumber halves.

11. Start rolling up the roll. Use the remaining white rice to fill any gaps before closing the roll.

12. Cut the roll into 4 pieces.

Rose Variation バラ

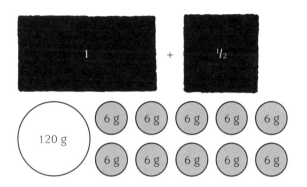

Ingredients

1 sheet + ¹/₂ sheet of seaweed, joined

2 egg sheets, each 19-cm x 9-cm

120 g white sushi rice

75 g pink sushi rice (60 g white sushi rice + 15 g pink fish flakes (*oboro*) (page 29)), divided into 12 parts, each approximately 6 g

6 slices salmon sashimi, cut into 12 small pieces

2 tsp flying fish roe (*tobiko*)

5 spinach stalks, each 10-cm long, blanched

1. Line a sushi mat with cling wrap and place an egg sheet on the mat.

2. Randomly place 6 salmon sashimi, 1 tsp roe and 6 parts pink rice on the egg sheet.

3. Using the cling wrap, roll the egg sheet up to create a spiral pattern. Set aside.

4. Repeat to randomly place the remaining salmon sashimi, roe and pink rice on the other egg sheet.

5. Place the egg roll from step 3 on the ingredients.

6. Using the cling wrap, roll the egg sheet up to enclose the egg roll.

7. Spread 120 g white rice on the 1 1/2 sheet of seaweed, leaving a 5-cm gap at one end.

8. Place the spinach stalks on the rice, keeping them apart.

9. Place the egg roll on the rice.

10. Using the sushi mat, roll up the sushi.

11. Cut the roll into 4 pieces.

Boy and Girl 男の子と女の子

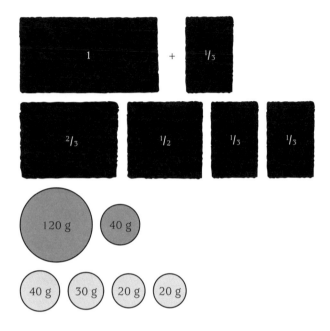

Ingredients

1 sheet + ⅓ sheet of seaweed, joined

1 x ⅔ sheet of seaweed

1 x ½ sheet of seaweed

2 x ⅓ sheet of seaweed

160 g black sushi rice (140 g white sushi rice + 20 g ground black sesame (*suri goma*)), divided

110 g light brown sushi rice (110 g white sushi rice + teriyaki sauce), divided

2 pickled gourd strips (*kanpyo*), each 10-cm x 2-cm

4 V-shape pieces of Japanese fish roll (*kamaboko*), pink part, for ribbons

4 curved lines of seaweed for mouths

1. Pat dry pickled gourd strips and wrap separately with $^1/_3$ sheet of seaweed.

2. Roll each one up tightly for the eyes. Set aside.

3. Shape 120 g black rice into a 10-cm long cylinder. Wrap with $^1/_2$ sheet of seaweed.

4. Using a knife, cut the roll lengthwise in half for the hair.

5. Place the roll cut-side down in the centre of the 1$^1/_3$ sheet of seaweed.

6. Spread 20 g light brown rice on each half-roll.

7. Using the sushi mat, bring the roll together. Press the light brown rice down so there are no gaps.

8. Top with 30 g light brown rice to start forming the shape of the face.

9. Place the pickled gourd strip eyes on the light brown rice.

10. Top with 40 g light brown rice, forming a mound so the face is round.

11. Close up the roll and cut into 4 pieces. Set aside.

12. To make ponytails, spread 40 g black rice on $^1/_2$ sheet seaweed, leaving a 1-cm gap at one end.

13. Fold the roll up and press on one side to form a teardrop shape roll.

14. Cut the teardrop shape roll into 4 pieces.

15. Assemble the ponytails and fish roll ribbons for the girl and finish with seaweed mouths.

Heart ハート

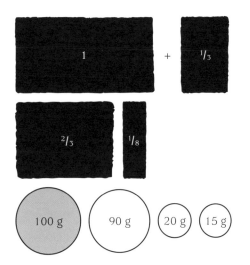

Ingredients

1 sheet + ¹/₃ sheet of seaweed, joined

1 x ²/₃ sheet of seaweed

1 x ¹/₈ sheet of seaweed

125 g white sushi rice

100 g pink sushi rice (85 g white sushi rice + 15 g pink fish floss (*sakura denbu*))

1. Shape 100 g pink rice into a 10-cm long cylinder.

2. Wrap with ²/₃ sheet of seaweed and use the sushi mat to shape the roll triangular.

3. Make a shallow cut on one side of the roll using a knife.

4. Fold the ¹/₈ sheet of seaweed lengthwise in half and place it into the cut to define the heart shape.

5. Fill the gap with 15 g white rice.

6. Spread 90 g white rice on the 1¹/₃ sheet of seaweed, leaving a 5-cm gap at each end.

7. Place the heart shape roll on the rice, cut-side down.

8. Start rolling up the roll. Use the remaining white rice to fill any gaps before closing the roll.

9. Cut the roll into 4 pieces.

Gift Box プレゼント

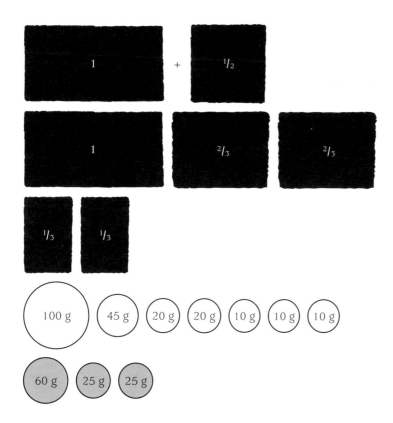

Ingredients

1 sheet + $^1/_2$ sheet of seaweed, joined

1 sheet of seaweed

2 x $^2/_3$ sheet of seaweed

2 x $^1/_3$ sheet of seaweed

2 strips of seaweed, each 10-cm x 1-cm

195 g white sushi rice, divided

110 g red sushi rice (95 g white sushi rice + 15 g chopped red ginger), divided

1 grilled omelette (*tamagoyaki*) (page 30)

1. Shape 60 g red rice into a 10-cm x 4-cm x 1-cm slab and wrap with ²/₃ sheet of seaweed for the ribbon.

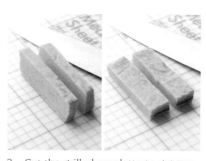

2. Cut the grilled omelette to get two 10-cm x 3-cm x 1-cm strips and two 10-cm x 2-cm x 1-cm strips.

3. Place the wrapped red rice and the two 10-cm x 3-cm x 1-cm omelette strips on 1 sheet of seaweed.

4. Wrap the ingredients with the seaweed and trim any excess seaweed. Set aside.

5. Place the remaining 2 omelette strips 1-cm apart on ²/₃ sheet of seaweed, for the top of the box.

6. Invert the wrapped ingredients on the omelette strips, with the red rice slab sitting in the gap.

7. Wrap the omelette strips with the seaweed.

8. Spread 20 g white rice on each side of the wrapped ingredients.

9. Spread 25 g red rice on ¹/₃ sheet of seaweed for the ribbon.

10. Place a strip of seaweed on one edge of rice.

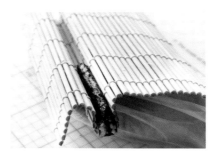

11. Fold the roll up and press on one side to form a teardrop shape roll. Repeat to make another roll.

12. Spread 100 g white rice on the 1 1/2 sheet of seaweed, leaving a 5-cm gap at each end.

13. Place the box in the centre, with the top of the box facing up.

14. Place the teardrop rolls on the box. Fill the 3 gaps around the rolls with 10 g white rice each.

15. Top with 45 g white rice and close up the roll.

16. Cut the roll into 4 pieces.

Stockists

Sushi-making Tools & Ingredients

Daiso
www.daisoglobal.com

Bento&co
www.bentoandco.com

BentoUSA
www.BentoUSA.com

Isetan
www.isetan.com.sg

Meidi-ya
www.meidi-ya.com.sg

Tokyu Hands
www.tokyu-hands.com.sg

Takashimaya
www.takashimaya.com.sg

Sushi Rice

Okome Shortgrain Rice
www.topseller.com.sg

Sushi Vinegar

Hinode Mirin
www.hinode-mirin.co.jp

Weights & Measures

Quantities for this book are given in Metric and American (spoon) measures. Standard spoon and cup measurements used are: 1 tsp = 5 ml, 1 Tbsp = 15 ml, 1 cup = 250 ml. All measures are level unless otherwise stated.

LIQUID AND VOLUME MEASURES

Metric	Imperial	American
5 ml	$^1/_6$ fl oz	1 teaspoon
10 ml	$^1/_3$ fl oz	1 dessertspoon
15 ml	$^1/_2$ fl oz	1 tablespoon
60 ml	2 fl oz	$^1/_4$ cup (4 tablespoons)
85 ml	$2^1/_2$ fl oz	$^1/_3$ cup
90 ml	3 fl oz	$^3/_8$ cup (6 tablespoons)
125 ml	4 fl oz	$^1/_2$ cup
180 ml	6 fl oz	$^3/_4$ cup
250 ml	8 fl oz	1 cup
300 ml	10 fl oz ($^1/_2$ pint)	$1^1/_4$ cups
375 ml	12 fl oz	$1^1/_2$ cups
435 ml	14 fl oz	$1^3/_4$ cups
500 ml	16 fl oz	2 cups
625 ml	20 fl oz (1 pint)	$2^1/_2$ cups
750 ml	24 fl oz ($1^1/_5$ pints)	3 cups
1 litre	32 fl oz ($1^3/_5$ pints)	4 cups
1.25 litres	40 fl oz (2 pints)	5 cups
1.5 litres	48 fl oz ($2^2/_5$ pints)	6 cups
2.5 litres	80 fl oz (4 pints)	10 cups

DRY MEASURES

Metric	Imperial
30 grams	1 ounce
45 grams	$1^1/_2$ ounces
55 grams	2 ounces
70 grams	$2^1/_2$ ounces
85 grams	3 ounces
100 grams	$3^1/_2$ ounces
110 grams	4 ounces
125 grams	$4^1/_2$ ounces
140 grams	5 ounces
280 grams	10 ounces
450 grams	16 ounces (1 pound)
500 grams	1 pound, $1^1/_2$ ounces
700 grams	$1^1/_2$ pounds
800 grams	$1^1/_2$ pounds
1 kilogram	2 pounds, 3 ounces
1.5 kilograms	3 pounds, $4^1/_2$ ounces
2 kilograms	4 pounds, 6 ounces

LENGTH

Metric	Imperial
0.5 cm	$^1/_4$ inch
1 cm	$^1/_2$ inch
1.5 cm	$^3/_4$ inch
2.5 cm	1 inch

ABBREVIATION

tsp	teaspoon
Tbsp	Tablespoon
g	gram
kg	kilogram
ml	millilitre